For AIDAN,

Dream Big!

KOKOPELLI
AND THE

TWO TRIBES

WRITTEN BY MICHAEL STERNS

Grasshopper dream productions

ILLUSTRATED BY
NATHAN HORODYSKY

LAYOUT BY
DUSTIN ROWLEY

Library of Congress Catalog Card Number: 2010902381
ISBN 978-0-615-35616-7

Printed at Everbest Printing Company in China
through Four Colour Print Group in Louisville, KY

Grasshopper Dream Productions
777 Claudia Lane
Palm Harbor, FL 34683

**Book orders: www.grasshopperdreams.com
813-382-4230**

Sterns, Michael.
    Kokopelli and the two tribes / by Michael Sterns;
    illustrated by Nathan Horodysky. -- 1st ed.
    SUMMARY: Kokopelli and Samsara quest for and find
    Samsara's lost tribe. The arrival of a Chief, once bad but
    turned good, and his tribe, creates conflict. The children help
    resolve the conflict and remind the two tribes of peace and
    forgiveness.
    Audience: Ages 4 and up.
    LCCN 2010902381
    ISBN 978-0-615-35616-7

Production Location: Everbest Printing Co., Guangdong, China
Production Date: 6/1/2010
Job/Batch Number: 94042

Dedicated to the book loving child in all of us...

When I was a child, I vividly recall spending time with my Grandma Fortin, and one of our favorite things to do was read books. All kinds of books! Grandma would choose from the simplest to the deepest of reads, and it was in the latter that my love of reading really took hold.

If you recall, Moms and Dads, the classic fairytales of yesteryear were not just little silly sound-bites that took five minutes to read... they were longer stories that might take two to three nights to get through! These stories were epic by today's standards, and that's a bit of a shame. You see, I loved those old books, because on a long weekend with Grandma she would read the one book over my entire stay. She would ask me questions like: "Where were we in the story, Mikey?" or "What do you think is going to happen next, Mikey?" Boy did that get my wheels turning! And what I really loved about those old books is that I didn't leave them behind like the sillier, shorter picture books. These were books to be read forevermore!

These were the books that elevated my reading comprehension years beyond my classmates, and what I have modeled my own books after. **My books will help your children become better readers, or give your already advanced readers the deeper read they crave!**

I purposely created my books (***Kokopelli & the Butterfly, Kokopelli and the Island of Change***, and you are now holding my third book in the series) so you can "picture-walk" them with a three or year old. By using the vivid, colorful, realistic illustrations to teach the meaning of the story, you will absolutely engage even a toddler. Ask them what they see and show them things you know they haven't learned yet! They will be riveted, and it will entice them into letting you read my books aloud to them at a much younger age than you thought possible!

My books are perfect to read over two to three nights for Pre-K and Kindergartners. Don't forget to use your fingertips to show them each word as you read it to them!

I also wanted to create books that the middle grade kids can read independently, gaining the required confidence they need for chapter books. Sometimes kids get caught in between leaving their silly, "kiddy" picture books behind, but chapter books can be too overwhelming for them to take on. Caught in the middle, these kids can become frustrated and abandon deeper reading! My books are a deeper read, but not overwhelming, perfect to springboard them into confident chapter book reading!

Finally, I didn't want my fifth graders to outgrow them, since my books deal with environmentalism, peace, and celebrating diversity! Why should a book be left behind just because it has illustrations in it? It shouldn't!

Lo and behold, I now have tens of thousands of my books in the hands of kids of ***all ages*** and they are going absolutely bonkers over them! So curl up with your child, no matter what their age, and enjoy ***Kokopelli and the Two Tribes***... a book modeled after the classic fairy tale, just like when we were kids!

Happy reading!
Michael Sterns, Author

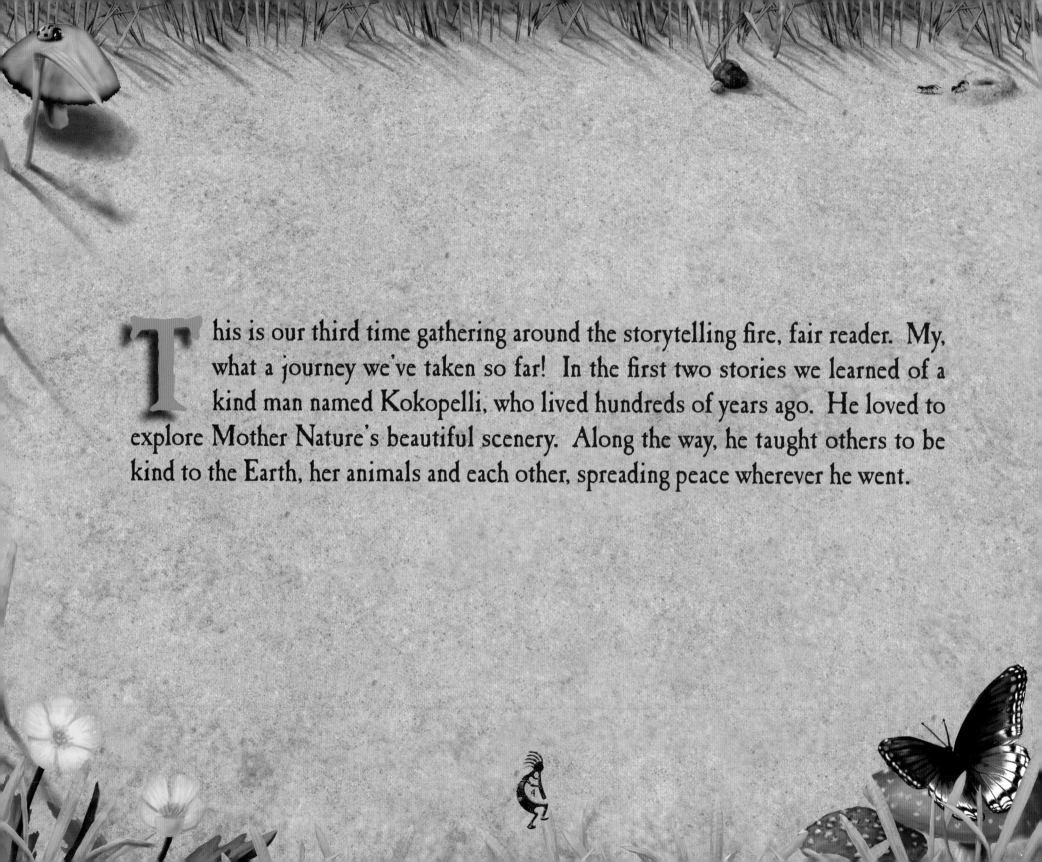

This is our third time gathering around the storytelling fire, fair reader. My, what a journey we've taken so far! In the first two stories we learned of a kind man named Kokopelli, who lived hundreds of years ago. He loved to explore Mother Nature's beautiful scenery. Along the way, he taught others to be kind to the Earth, her animals and each other, spreading peace wherever he went.

I f you recall, he once met a cruel chief who kept a gorgeous butterfly in a cage, and Kokopelli could see the poor creature inside was terribly sick and very frightened.

Kokopelli begged the chief to allow him to set the butterfly free into nature. The chief became furious and ordered his men to seize Kokopelli and the butterfly!

Being a peaceful man, Kokopelli refused to fight. He ran away with the butterfly to save its life, and his own.

He ran all day until sunset, and when he put the cage down, the forest's animals gathered around to watch the splendid butterfly fly free. The butterfly instantly healed, creating a gorgeous twinkling rainbow as it flew far away toward the setting sun.

The next day, the animals gathered again and introduced Kokopelli to their best friend. Her name was Samsara, and she was the most kind and gentle woman Kokopelli ever met. Samsara had the most amazing eyes, glowing with all the colors of the rainbow... the same colors as the wings of the butterfly!

Samsara told Kokopelli her incredible story. When she was a child, Samsara accidentally wandered from her family and became lost. The animals found her, and raised her peacefully. Even though Samsara missed her tribe very much, she spent many happy years with her new animal family. The cruel chief found Samsara playing with her wolf family, and feared her because she acted differently. He saw her rainbow colored eyes and feared Samsara even more because she looked differently too!

Her differences caused the chief to fear she was a bad spirit. So he ordered his medicine man to cast a spell on Samsara, transforming her into a butterfly! That way, the chief could keep her in a cage and feel safe. Had the chief only communicated with her, he would have realized Samsara was as sweet as could be. When Kokopelli opened the cage door twenty years later, he broke that terrible spell and saved Samsara's life.

Kokopelli and Samsara fell deeply in love with each other that day. Soon, Samsara searched out and found the chief who ordered the spell cast upon her, because she needed to forgive him. She forgave Chief Sleeping Bear because she knew his father taught him those cruel ways when the chief was a child. Forgiven and changed for the better, Chief Sleeping Bear presided over Kokopelli and Samsara's wedding. Soon after, the happy couple was off to explore the world together!

And that, fair reader, is where their new adventure begins...

One lovely summer day, Kokopelli and Samsara were sitting together, enjoying the breathtaking scenery that surrounded them. Many of their animal friends were nearby, nibbling on flowers and relaxing in the warm sunlight. Because Kokopelli and Samsara were so kind to the animals, they were all like family, and they enjoyed each other's company very much.

Kokopelli could see there was something troubling Samsara, and he listened quietly and attentively as she told him what was on her mind.

"Kokopelli, I miss my real family very much. I have thought of them every day since I lost them so long ago. I would like to find them so we might all be together again" she explained. "Would you help me, even though the journey might be long and difficult?" she asked.

Kokopelli loved Samsara with all of his heart and soul. "Samsara, I would follow you to the ends of the Earth on this quest!" he exclaimed. "Together we will find your lost tribe. This is my promise to you."

With happy tears rolling down her face, Samsara and Kokopelli hugged each other. Then they began the preparation for this remarkable journey to find Samsara's tribe.

Kokopelli and Samsara knew that to accomplish a goal, one should always have a plan and not be afraid to ask other people for help. They also knew that whenever one is on a quest, it's better to have fun along the way! They decided that while looking for Samsara's tribe, they would be sure to enjoy the fantastic scenery that Mother Nature provided. They also knew they would meet many other interesting tribes while traveling. There would be good days and bad days, but sharing smiles with different people would certainly make this difficult quest more enjoyable.

They carefully planned their expedition, organizing and packing the essential supplies. They encouraged each other as they prepared to depart upon this trip of a lifetime.

Samsara remembered from her childhood that her family loved to travel and explore, and moved around quite often. Unable to guess where her family could be now, Samsara and Kokopelli decided to begin their quest in a place they always wanted to visit themselves. They figured they might as well explore new areas while searching, making the journey even more fun!

They began their trip in the region we now call the Florida Everglades. The chief of the tribe they met here had once met Samsara's Grandmother, the Medicine Woman of her tribe. He told stories of this powerful, friendly Medicine Woman and her ability to heal the sick. This was many, many moons ago, however, in the far off mountain range to the north.

Kokopelli and Samsara made many new friends in this tribe, and after thanking the chief, they left to find the mountains he described.

Next their travels took them to what are now called the Appalachian Mountains, also known as the "Smoky Mountains". Here they met a tribe that had last seen Samsara's family far to the west, two summers before. The couple spent several days enjoying the spectacular scenery, the variety of interesting plants and animals, and the company of this kind tribe. Well rested, they began their long trip to the west.

Kokopelli and Samsara traveled great distances toward the sunset. Soon they reached a breathtaking "Grand Canyon", in a land now called Arizona. The tribe here had traded goods with Samsara's family just four seasons ago, not too far to the north.

amsara and Kokopelli wound through the valleys, forests and majestic peaks of what is now called the Rocky Mountain chain in beautiful Colorado. Here they encountered a tribe that met Samsara's father during the previous autumn, in the desert to the west.

Soon they found themselves in the high desert, among the most unusual red rock formations they had ever seen. In a land now known as Arches National Park in Moab, Utah, a tribe told of meeting Samsara's family to the northwest during the thawing of the previous snow.

Kokopelli and Samsara trekked to a strange land that breathed steam! They were in the wondrous territory we now call Yellowstone National Park. They saw plumes of steam, boiling mud pits and clear emerald colored hot springs everywhere.

The tribe they met here had participated in a ceremony with Samsara's family just weeks before! They knew where her tribe's camp was to the west!

Their quest finally over, Samsara shrieked with joy as she caught sight of her family picking flowers in a beautiful meadow, just as they had been the day she lost them so long ago. Kokopelli laughed as he watched his beloved Samsara running like a little girl toward her long lost family. He could see the looks of happiness and disbelief on their faces.

Kokopelli could hear his wife calling out "It's me, Samsara!" As she approached, they began to run toward her. Soon they were in a pile hugging, kissing, smiling and laughing. Tears of happiness streamed down all their faces.

He gave them a little time to get reacquainted, and was so proud of his wife for accomplishing her goal. Samsara excitedly invited Kokopelli over to meet her family, and the hugging began again.

The tribe gathered around the fire to learn about what happened to Samsara. The last time they saw her she was just a five year old little girl.

They heard how Samsara became lost that fateful day, and how the animals had raised her peacefully and lovingly. She told how Chief Sleeping Bear and his tribe mistakenly feared she was a bad spirit because she was found playing with wolves and had rainbow colored eyes. They were afraid of her just because she looked and acted differently! She shuddered, recalling how the Chief's medicine man cast the spell on her, transforming her into a butterfly so they could cage her.

Kokopelli told of finding her as a suffering butterfly in a cage and setting her free. They told Samsara's family how opening the cage broke the terrible spell, saving her life. Her tribe smiled, hearing how Samsara and Kokopelli fell deeply in love with each other that fateful day.

Together they told the tribe how they had forgiven the Chief when they learned he had been taught those cruel ways as a child. They explained how Chief Sleeping Bear changed into a good man and actually presided over their wedding ceremony!

The next day, there was a feast beyond all feasts to celebrate Samsara's return. Kokopelli was immediately treated as one of the family, and the happy couple spent hours talking and laughing with her tribe. They ate lovingly prepared, delicious food and watched the children of the tribe playing games.

Samsara's family tended to her constantly, treating her as if she were a forest princess.

Four seasons passed, and Kokopelli enjoyed becoming part of Samsara's tribe very much. Like him, they were very kind to the forest's animals. The tribe treated these creatures as if they were part of the family. The animals were always grazing or frolicking about, much to the delight of the tribe.

The tribe also always took care to keep the land and water clean, and treated each other with equal kindness. They discussed their problems gently, always seeking a peaceful resolution.

One day, Kokopelli and Samsara happily told the tribe they were expecting the birth of a new baby!

ittle did they know that they would soon have twin babies, a boy and a girl! They gave their baby girl the name of Breeze. Hawk was the name given to their baby boy.

Samsara and Kokopelli were wonderful parents, teaching their twins kindly and sharing much laughter.

Hawk and Breeze were inseparable, always providing the tribe with hilarious entertainment!

The twins were naturally quite curious and loved to learn. Kokopelli and Samsara always taught Breeze and Hawk that learning is fun and important. Through their actions, the twins constantly reminded the adults of the tribe to remain curious.

It was in the spring of the twins' sixth year that another tribe approached, and the two tribes would be changed forever.

For just across the river, it happened to be Chief Sleeping Bear's tribe that drew near! Kokopelli and Samsara immediately recognized the chief and his people. Splashing through the water with huge smiles upon their faces, they ran toward Chief Sleeping Bear as fast as they could. It was obvious to all that Kokopelli, Samsara, and the Chief were great friends despite their past problems.

The three embraced each other, and soon the introductions were made between the two tribes.

36

As was the custom in Samsara's tribe, Chief Sleeping Bear and his people were invited to join in a welcoming feast and fireside chat.

Kokopelli could sense a problem. Most of Samsara's tribe remained in conversation among themselves, not including Chief Sleeping Bear's tribe in the talks. He noticed that many of the chief's men quickly retired to their own fires across the river. He also noticed that Samsara's parents quickly excused themselves to their own hut.

For the first time in many years, it appeared that trouble had once again returned to the two tribes.

S amsara's parents closed the door to their hut, and lit a small fire to discuss what was bothering them. Her father, Chief Dancing Elk, spoke first, with an upset expression on his face. Her mother, Peaceful Dove, listened attentively as he spoke.

"It brings much pain to my heart to meet the man who ordered the spell cast upon our daughter so many years ago. I know she and Kokopelli forgave Chief Sleeping Bear, and it is obvious they are friends. However, I cannot yet forgive this man who cost our daughter so many years of her life", said Chief Dancing Elk.

"I too am bothered by this man's presence", Peaceful Dove replied. "Although forgiveness is something we have always taught our children, I struggle to forgive the man who ordered our Samsara to be transformed into a butterfly and caged", she said.

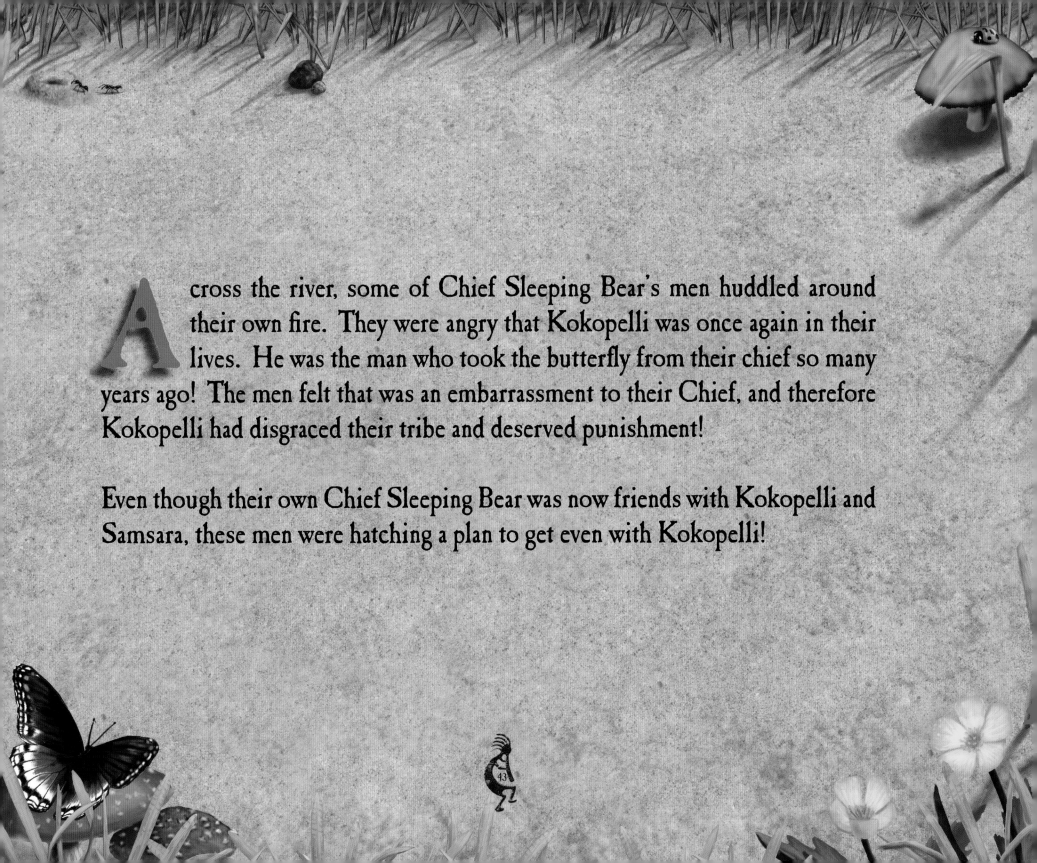

Across the river, some of Chief Sleeping Bear's men huddled around their own fire. They were angry that Kokopelli was once again in their lives. He was the man who took the butterfly from their chief so many years ago! The men felt that was an embarrassment to their Chief, and therefore Kokopelli had disgraced their tribe and deserved punishment!

Even though their own Chief Sleeping Bear was now friends with Kokopelli and Samsara, these men were hatching a plan to get even with Kokopelli!

43

The next day, Kokopelli took these same men of Chief Sleeping Bear's tribe on an expedition to show them where they could find food and supplies for their tribe. Kokopelli could sense they were angry with him, and he correctly guessed it had to do with his rescuing the butterfly from their Chief so long ago.

What he did not realize is that these men had a plan for revenge. They thought it would be funny to push Kokopelli while one of them crouched on the ground behind him. Keenly aware, Kokopelli saw this at the last moment. Instead of falling on his back the way the men intended, he stayed on his feet and tripped backward.

As Kokopelli stumbled he clutched at some small tree branches to regain his balance, but they broke off in his hand. The men stared in horror as Kokopelli fell over the edge of the canyon wall! At the last moment, Kokopelli grabbed onto some roots protruding between the rocks at the top of the cliff, swinging hundreds of feet above the valley floor below!

The men quickly grabbed Kokopelli's arms and pulled him back to safety. Embarrassed and frightened, they explained how it was supposed to be a harmless prank, and then ran back to their camp.

44

Kokopelli took a few deep breaths, grateful to be alive. As he walked back to his camp, he thought about what just happened. The first emotion he felt was anger at how careless and mean-spirited those men were. Breathing deeply again, he then realized what these men had been thinking about him and why.

He understood their point of view. Although he didn't agree with their response, he could see why they did what they did, and he knew he would forgive them.

As he strolled back into his camp, Kokopelli could hear the men admitting what they had done and begging Chief Sleeping Bear's forgiveness. He could also see a sad look on Samsara's face as she talked to her parents about their bad feelings toward Chief Sleeping Bear. Kokopelli looked around, noticing many upset faces among the two tribes.

Kokopelli knew it was time to ask the elders for help.

Kokopelli called a meeting of Samsara, her parents, Samsara's Grandmother the Medicine Woman, Chief Sleeping Bear, and his Medicine Man. The Medicine Man and Medicine Woman were very important people. They were the elders the tribes people called upon when someone was sick and needed healing, or when a serious problem needed to be solved.

They gathered around the fire, and Kokopelli spoke first. He brought the problems of both tribes into the open, and the wise old Medicine Man and Woman nodded their heads in understanding as he talked.

The elder man and woman agreed these problems were indeed serious, and decided to work together to solve them. They both thought it best to get a good night's sleep and approach this crisis with fresh minds in the morning.

The wise old Medicine Woman and Medicine Man awakened early the next day, with a gorgeous sunrise painting the sky. They agreed that a walk through Mother Nature's beauty might bring them inspiration on how to bring the tribes together.

They walked on, speaking gently to each other and exchanging ideas. They enjoyed the breathtakingly beautiful sights surrounding them. The animals were all around, as if they were listening in on this important conversation. The old man and woman walked through the forest and along the river bank. They strolled under the shadow of gigantic cliffs, and looked out over stunning vistas from great heights.

They stopped occasionally to enjoy snacks of delicious berries, nuts and fruits. The Medicine Man kindly brought water from the river to his new friend. She smiled at him as she graciously accepted. It was obvious these two liked each other very much!

51

Hours later, the Medicine Man and Woman approached the split camps, noticing how they were clearly separated by the river. Although they shared intense conversation all day, they still did not feel any closer to a solution that would heal the tribes' problems and bring their people together.

As they drew nearer, they noticed both tribes' children playing together. From toddlers to teenagers, the boys and girls splashed in the river, played games, and were all laughing and shouting. The children knew nothing of the adults' problems or the separation between the two tribes. They were too busy being curious, having fun, exploring, and interacting peacefully together!

The Medicine Woman looked at the Medicine Man, smiled and said "I believe we have found the answer to our problem".

The Medicine Man smiled back and nodded. They agreed to gather the tribes together, and meet back at that same spot immediately.

Listening respectfully to the Medicine Man and Woman's request, the two tribes quickly gathered at the river, naturally forming a circle around the playing children. The youngsters smiled and continued playing, as if to teach the adults the lesson they needed to learn.

Kokopelli smiled as he noticed the Medicine Man and Woman holding hands, the affection between them obvious. The Medicine Woman cleared her throat and the children stopped playing and the tribes became silent. She nodded at the Medicine Man, who smiled and nodded back at her.

"It has come to our attention that the past has created problems between our two tribes, where there should be peace, instead. This great Medicine Woman and I have been in counsel all day so we might find a way to bring love into all of our hearts. The answer is right in front of you", the Medicine Man boomed while waving his hand toward the children.

Then the Medicine Woman said "Kokopelli, Samsara and Chief Sleeping Bear forgave each other long ago, becoming the best of friends. It is time everyone else does the same. Look at these children in front of you! They know nothing of your anger, separation and vengeance. Surely we have much to learn from their ability to love unconditionally! For the sake of the children, and their children, I ask you to look into each other's eyes, offering and seeking forgiveness".

The men and women of the two tribes looked at the children, then at each other, and their concerned and upset expressions melted away, quickly replaced by warm smiles.

The once angry men of Chief Sleeping Bear's tribe approached Kokopelli, and he extended his arms toward them in a gesture of peace. They embraced, with huge grins upon their faces as forgiveness settled into their hearts.

Peaceful Dove and Dancing Elk approached Chief Sleeping Bear, and the three of them hugged and laughed.

Kokopelli and Samsara gazed lovingly into each other's eyes, sharing a gentle kiss and hug. They then turned to look at the Medicine Woman and Medicine Man, who were lovingly gazing into each other's eyes.

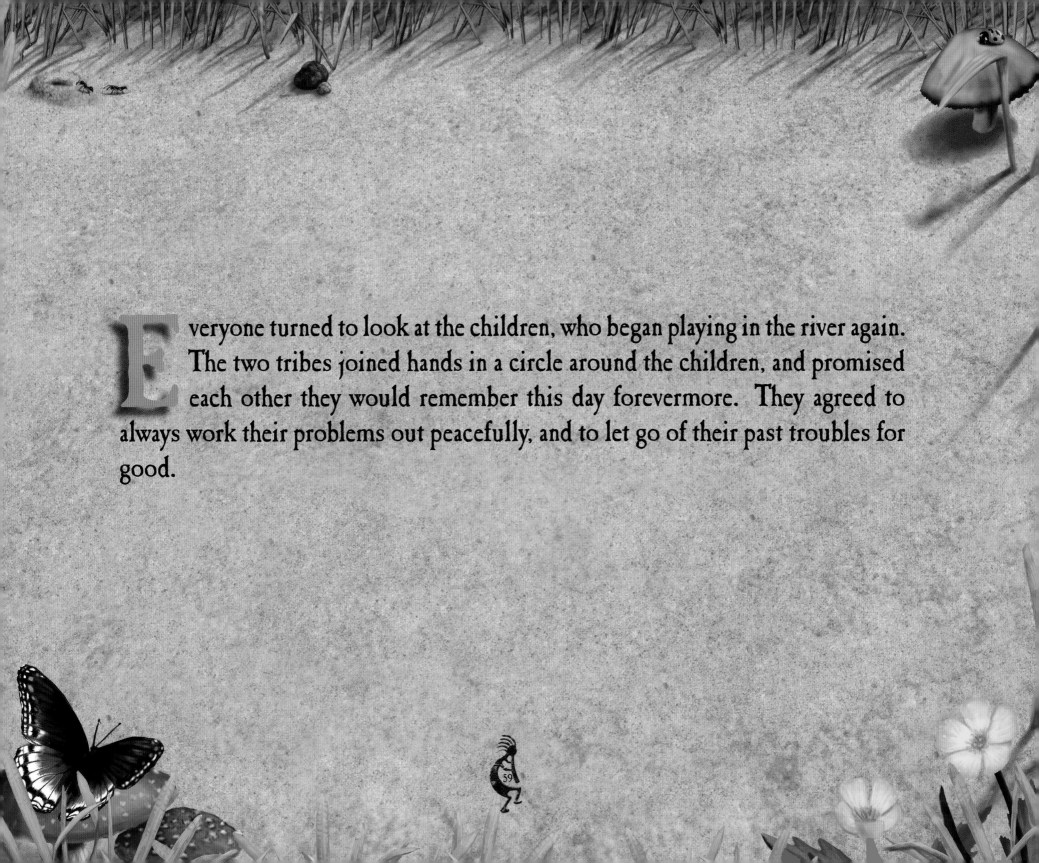

Everyone turned to look at the children, who began playing in the river again. The two tribes joined hands in a circle around the children, and promised each other they would remember this day forevermore. They agreed to always work their problems out peacefully, and to let go of their past troubles for good.

That night, with all forgiven, the two tribes gathered in each other's camps. Everyone laughed, sang, told stories and ate delicious food around each other's campfires.

Kokopelli, Samsara, Dancing Elk, Peaceful Dove, Chief Sleeping Bear, and the Medicine Man and Woman mingled, feeling as if the two tribes were now one big, happy tribe. They shared food, conversation, hugs and smiles as they danced under the moon and stars.

That night, the two tribes slept more peacefully than they ever had in their entire lives. Snuggled in their beds like happy children, they all called out "Good night!" to each other, their kind voices echoing off the canyon walls and into the forest.

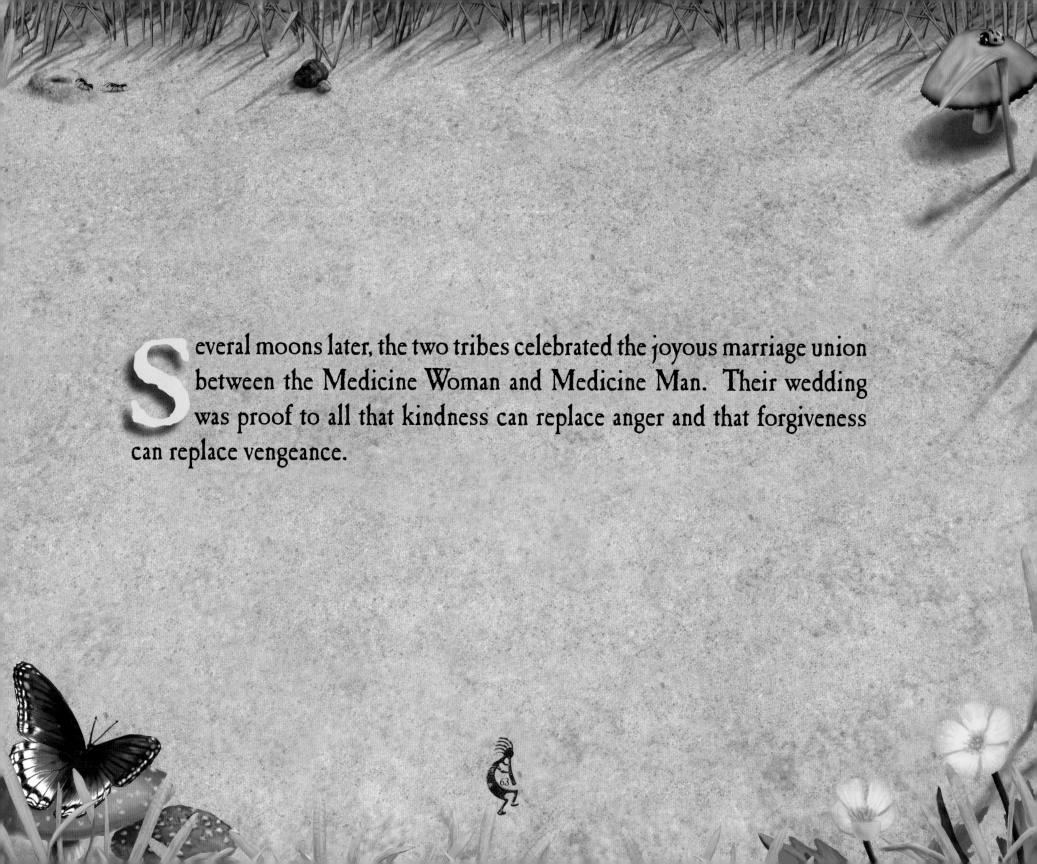

Several moons later, the two tribes celebrated the joyous marriage union between the Medicine Woman and Medicine Man. Their wedding was proof to all that kindness can replace anger and that forgiveness can replace vengeance.

It has been a few years since the two tribes met along the river. Love has bloomed among them, and the two tribes have now become one growing, peaceful tribe. They all lived happily ever after... *because of the children.*